Arab In newsland

Lena Khalaf Tuffaha

Winner of the 2016 Two Sylvias Press Chapbook Prize

Two Sylvias Press

To Irv's
Best
Wishes

3/17

Two Sylvias Press
PO Box 1524
Kingston, WA 98346
twosylviaspress@gmail.com

Cover Design: Kelli Russell Agodon
Book Design: Annette Spaulding-Convy
2016 Chapbook Prize Judge: January Gill O'Neil
Author Photo Credit: Reema Tuffaha

Created with the belief that great writing is good for the world, Two Sylvias Press mixes modern technology, classic style, and literary intellect with an eco-friendly heart. We draw our inspiration from the poetic literary talent of Sylvia Plath and the editorial business sense of Sylvia Beach. We are an independent press dedicated to publishing the exceptional voices of writers.

For more information about Two Sylvias Press or to learn more about the eBook version of *Arab In Newsland* please visit: www.twosylviaspress.com

First Edition. Created in the United States of America.

ISBN: 978-0-9986314-9-3

Two Sylvias Press
www.twosylviaspress.com

Praise For *Arab In Newsland*

Whenever she turns on the "never good news," Lena Khalaf Tuffaha sees her relatives in Syria, Jordan, and Palestine in pain and turmoil. She sees beloved cities blasted to rubble. She knows that "when darkness arrives the blue glow / of screens will bring you no warmth." What does allow us refuge is her beating heart, her wide and generous intelligence. These poems take us deep into the inside story of devastation and despair. These poems make us more human. Lena Khalaf Tuffaha's brilliant poems are gifts of grace.
　— **Peggy Shumaker**, author of *Toucan Nest: Poems of Costa Rica*

Acknowledgements

Thank you to January Gill O'Neil and to Kelli Russell Agodon and Annette Spaulding-Convy for publishing *Arab in Newsland*.

Thank you to the mentors at Rainier Writing Workshop whose wisdom and kindness helped to bring the best versions of these poems into the world: Peggy Shumaker, Oliver de la Paz, and Rick Barot.

Thank you to my sister poets, Molly Spencer and Billie Swift, the best companions on this poetry journey.

Gratitude to Ahmad and Osama, sunshine of my childhood and best friends in adulthood, and to my parents, for their love and for their stories. There aren't enough words for the love I have for Naseem, Raya, Reema, and Renda.

Gratitude to the editors of the following journals for publishing some of the poems in this chapbook:

"Lullaby" published by *Indianola Review*, Fall 2016, and nominated for a Pushcart Prize.

"Maritime Nocturne" published in *Gaza Unsilenced* by Just World Books, July 2015.

"*(Dis)placed: Found Poems of the War in Syria*" published by *James Franco Review*, September 2015.

"As In" published by *Seattle Review of Books,* July 2016.

"Solidarity" published by *Crab Creek Review*, Winter 2017.

"Bleu Blanc Rouge" published by *Pittsburgh Poetry Review*, February 2016.

"Future Perfect" published as an Inaugural response poem in *The Rumpus,* January 2017.

"Nakba" published by *diode,* March 2016.

"In Case of Emergency" forthcoming from *Massachusetts Review,* Winter 2017.

"When the Sky is No Longer a Womb" published by *Compose,* April 2016.

Mawwal is an Arabic song form, usually a solo performance without music, featuring a repeated line.

Nakba is an Arabic word meaning "catastrophe." It is the name Palestinians have given to their dispossession and the loss of their homeland beginning in in 1948.

Table of Contents

For Naseem
حبيبي

LULLABY

We cannot carry you,
our arms warm and dry
too late at the shore
of what has cradle-fallen
what sent a woman who fears the sea
what sent a man who fears the burning
skies of his country
into the razor-edged waves.

We cannot carry you,
tiny boat capsized,
upturned fish floating
in the glass bowl of our screens.

We cannot carry you.
We sink deeper, beyond
the midnight zone.
How to measure the trenches
of our silence, little one?

We want things smaller than we know.
A vessel strong enough
to lift you into tomorrow,
a life jacket or two,
a pair of small shoes
pressing into the sand.

MARITIME NOCTURNE

Across the sea floor
limbs curl through ink clouds,

settle near an old trunk
spilling its treasures.

Sodden maps surrender
their borders and silver frames

tarnish. Currents swallow
dark clots and across Gaza the rain

sorties over new monuments
of ash, open wounds of rubble.

Waves buckle under
the weight of swollen

vessels, flayed carcass, hauling
hundreds of lives

to shorelines where no one
looks forward to their arrival,

relentless survivors, white-knuckle
grasping at stars, reaching

for the buckle of Orion's
belt, cleft of his boot.

Even on nights when
there is no anchor, the brine

of a dream consumed

by the sea, salt like shards
on parched lips is gentler

than the sulfur of prayer—
the dry scorch of waiting for mercy.

TIMELINE

What's on your mind?

M shared the Syria Campaign's photo.
N invited you to play Candy Crush Saga.
It's O's birthday today. Help them celebrate!
P commented on a post you shared.
Q replied to P's comment.
25 people liked your post.

What's on your mind?

N tagged you in a picture.
N invited you to play Candy Crush Saga.
P changed her profile picture.
N added three photos from last night.
O is marked safe in Paris.
M shared #Aleppo is Burning's photo.
Q and three others commented on M's photo.
N shared a photo to your Timeline.
It's P's birthday. Help them celebrate!
Q changed her relationship status.
M was attending Fundraiser for Syria's Children.
O invited you to play Candy Crush Saga.
R is marked safe in Brussels.
S likes your comment on her post.
You and T have 8 friends in common.

We care about your memories. Here's a post from 8 years ago.

It's International Hairstyle Day. Share your most memorable hairstyle.
M shared a picture from #Aleppo is Burning.
236 people reacted. Sad faces. Angry faces.
Click here to see more comments.

(DIS)PLACED: FOUND POEMS FROM THE WAR IN SYRIA

Zaatari Refugee Camp
We used to dream about snow.
It was like a fairytale.
But that was when we had shoes
and our feet were warm inside our houses.

Damascus
The teacher told them they were
too loud. They needed to behave.
She sent them out of the classroom
for being bad. The barrel descended
from the sky exploding
in the school yard.
She hasn't stopped wailing,
they will never be loud again.

Yarmouk Refugee Camp
I don't remember what jam tastes like
but I know I used to love it.
We haven't even had bread for weeks
but I keep dreaming of apricot jam.
We haven't had water.

Beirut International Airport
Everyone said: "Why would a girl
do this?"
My brother and I are leaving.
In Sweden they grant some people asylum.
It's a really long journey

but it can't be worse than the war.
My friend is going
to film everything on his mobile phone.

Desert
Someone said they were a free army
from Libya. They wanted more money,
they wanted dollars,
sold us to other smugglers.
We couldn't argue; they scared us
with their guns. We didn't know
which country we were in. The desert
looks the same everywhere.
No one knows where we'll go
if they let us leave. They make us
wait
for trucks to take us to the sea.

Mediterranean Sea
And they kept bringing people
and more people and more people.
The boat rocked right to left and filled
with water. The smugglers told us
there would be life
jackets for everyone
but they lied. Everyone prays so
loud, so many shouting Allahu Akbar
because we know that now is finally
the moment we will die.

Italian Coast Guard Boat
My mother saw it on the news, the bodies
floating in the sea. She kept looking
for me and my brother. I thought

we would be happy
to survive but our friends drowned.
I don't know what to do now
that we are alive.

AS IN

On the plane I whisper the travel prayer more softly
I mouth the words but keep the breath carefully
concealed in my throat, worried I don't have a permit
for these verses in international airspace.

The prayer is filled with soft sounds—
Ash-ha-du   a silken hush, unlike
the sharp hiss of *testify*. And the mess
of vowels   *la ilaa ha illaa*   wants breath.
It is difficult to keep this all inside.
It is difficult to pray and even more
difficult to marvel or to rage.

Allah was my go-to word
for all the moments of the day
the wonders
as in
(close your eyes and savor here)
Allaaaaah   can you believe the fragrance of this gardenia?
the colors of this sunset? How is it your lips
are still as sweet as the first time?

And the transgressions
as in
(clench your fists and tremble here)
Allahu akbar!
Please help me survive this
Please help me believe this will end
Please help me trust there is some power
greater than all this suffering.

SOLIDARITY

It always begins with a question.
The person facing you may not realize
a neon halo shimmers
above her head as she gropes for evidence.

How the room you're in becomes
the interrogation chamber,
how she is comfortable
beneath the single distended bulb,
your life a file with claims
for her to evaluate.
I'm having trouble believing any woman
would choose that.

Woman from inside of what could be
the closest embrace,
our same bodies shamed, hunted.
How quickly the sound of our heartbeats
is smothered by the color of our skin.

A chorus assures you
she means no harm, this asking
for evidence, this lusting for what
aches inside of you.

A chorus assures you
she does not need you broken,
does not need a wound,
only the trickle of blood.

If you refuse to relinquish
what little is left of you,
if you refuse to extract the shrapnel,
slow dance of scar tissue in front of her,
then how can she empathize?

A chorus admonishes you
to disrobe, cross the bridge
into another country
an ocean apart from your kin.

Let the veil fall around
your shoulders,
only the flash of your hair can prove
you're one of us.

A chorus challenges you to
name the dead, list
their proximity to your heart,
describe the shape
and darkness of your bruises.

Only the ravishment of flesh
feeds our desire to love you
in spite of everything you are.

ANNIVERSARY

You are inside the calendar.

You are tiny font above the words
First Quarter Moon, under a double-digit,
two slender lines or two buildings you hadn't visited
before a storm speaking your language
took them down.

You are inside the calendar.

Your name is trapped in that one square
on a grid crowded with gaping white space
and faraway deaths that you remember, too,
like later in the month
when the women of Sabra and Shatila walked through
mounds of dead husbands and sons
saying, *I am the stranger, I have no one.*
You are of no earth, extraterrestrial. Another planet
best viewed on a screen.

You are inside the calendar.

A line cuts across this day
which you aren't allowed to grieve
and must always disavow,
the morning the prayer was stolen
from your throat and
you remember running to the front porch
to tear the first birthday balloons away
so no one would misunderstand
or imagine that you heart
isn't breaking, that you aren't afraid.

You are inside the calendar

that has an American sense of humor
and the words Happy Eid
are written in a child's purple marker
across the square marked September 11, 2016.

How to celebrate? Will there be balloons?

BLEU BLANC ROUGE

I can tell you what I have learned—
when darkness arrives the blue glow

of screens will bring you no warmth. You light candles
while the streets beyond you burn and the ashes

of other monuments thicken
the white skies of winter.

When will you understand that storm clouds
cannot be held back by borders?

Corpses pile up in trenches of parched clay,
flies swarm over stagnant hope and blood

no one ever washes out of limestone.
But the flames redden your eyes, your molars

grind down on my name like stale bread.
I would embrace you,

but I remember the thinness of skin
freshly bruised. I would tell you a story

but the salt searing through my wounds is loud
and I wish this medicine on no one.

I will wave all the flags you want
even though they are nothing but thread.

In the country where I was a child,
white shrouds outnumber night-colored banners.

We have only flesh, while it lives,
oxygen bluing our veins as it passes

through the red chambers of a beating
heart, a refuge where we can begin again.

I try not to think about the animal

on the road as my car approaches

no chance of slowing down   stopping
is out of the question   the lives

that would be compromised
ensuing despair   and it is already dead

my grief absurd in its delay
a useless luxury inside my climate-

controlled machine burning black gold
as it accelerates   I try

not to think about the animal
rearranged in unnatural configuration

its head visible in profile   one eye
refracting the last light it glimpsed

one limb
reaching out from ribbons

of entrails   fine circuitry
of skeleton cratered   loosened flesh

and fibers red blazing red
on an asphalt canvas   I try

not to think about the city
collapsing   buildings that held

the pulsing heart of life
the length of its branching streets

arteries of story   I try
not to think about how a city

besieged   battered   barrel-bombed
is its own animal

the mammoth weight
of man-made disaster   useless luxury of airstrikes

ordered from climate-controlled rooms
the absurdity of grief for its dismembered

limbs   burning limbs
staining its now-gray topography

its new monuments   how all cities collapsing
like animals on the road look the same

I try not to think
about human beings as animals

how there is no turning back
once the mind perceives a howl

as beastly   a wilderness to be tamed
I try not to think about

the disapproving click
of my grandmother's tongue

for this comparison   the kohl-rimmed oceans
of her eyes darkening   the absurdity

of finding the memory of her jasmine
songs   her brocade stories

in the carcass on the road
I try not to think

about the useless luxury of this side
of the world where animals are named

and cherished   their deaths mourned
their natural habitats

safe-guarded   their lives protected
alongside the absurdity of our own   I try

not to think about the logic
offered as fuel to keep me driving

that human history and the kingdom
of animal life paved

with our own gray symmetries
have cycles   that the body

in the rubble or on the road
should not be examined too closely

but in context of a motion
forward   birth pangs of what comes next

blood
loss

inevitable   I try
not to think about how my singular task

on this road might be to avoid driving over
the life already taken   I try not to think

about the useless luxury of someone else
tasked with cleaning this up

the maximum discomfort
I will endure on my climate-controlled journey

will be to look or to avoid looking
useless luxury of voyeurism   absurdity of witness

that a city   a life collapsed in this way
can have dignity in my gaze upon its death

I try not to hear my grandmother's voice
my grandmother who rarely spoke in hatred

but when on occasion news overwhelmed
absurdity of what never stopped unfolding

from deep inside her throat   a bile
would rise   her gums receding in its acrid flood

Animals   an epithet and
her only explanation for the useless luxury

of men failing her cities
collapsing the fine circuitry of a road forward

for the absurdity of our grief
that saves not one single life

I try not think about my grandmother
whose kohl-rimmed eyes faded slowly

my grandmother who watched the news even
as her tears abandoned her   her eyes sought refuge in darkness

news that is never more than old wounds
unsutured   hemorrhaging   I try not

to think of the now unfathomable luxury
of a natural death   that what she witnessed

in a lifetime of wars was just one wound
I try not to think about an animal rage

unleashed in her homeland   I try
not to think   a useless luxury

this grief   red square on a screen
in a gray expanse   an animal cry

collapse of language
heart failure   a wilderness

FUTURE PERFECT

When I was young Peter Jennings had a voice
like my parents' cigarettes
comfort of a familiar burning
fragrance of nightly never good news reports.

I learned that in America
I didn't have to take Peter's word
for anything. Tom and Dan and other people
on news stations that never slept
would tell me some version of what was happening.
But no one seemed to translate what the women were saying
or to film anything that looked familiar.

The country where my father learned
to grill fish by the riverbank
became Eye-rack
a dark place
pockmarked with green lights
on a TV screen in my American living room.

At school some teachers talked about protests.
There was a Mass at St. James and someone at the University
threw red paint to make people think of blood.
After the first week of war
prayers changed from *give peace a chance*
to *pray for our troops*.
There was so much country music.

When I was old enough I voted for a President I was sure
would never turn another country into a video game.
Then I learned about no-fly-zone trickle-down wars
fought on the margins of maps.
People found quiet ways to die off-screen
to live the slow burn of hunger
searing of malignancies for which no medication was allowed.

Someone asked the first female Secretary of State,
the one my feminist friends admired
if she felt it was worthwhile
that over half a million children
had died in the non-war we were waging.

She had a way
the Secretary who wore bedazzled brooches
of ruby-eyed serpents and eagles with sallow pearls in their bellies
she had a way of curling her upper lip
and settling into her chair
of hardening her jaw and saying *Yes.*

When Peter and Tom and Dan said
it appeared inevitable
that we were going to war again
in the same place for new reasons
I began to think of war as a season—
I knew what clothes to wear
what signs to put out in the yard.

I remember believing that evening streets full of protestors
and the Seattle Peace Choir singing on 6th Avenue
were my new country and my friends' kuffiyehs were its flag.
I remember the sound of my own voice chanting. Sometimes
the world we believe in distracts us. Sometimes
we aren't listening closely
noting the verb tenses.

Decisions have already been made.
Peter and Tom and Dan and all the smoky-toned storytellers
were just reading eulogies.

111

At home there was a simple answer
to *Where are we from?* for which the permanent
one hundred and eleven inscribed
between my father's thick eyebrows was punctuation.

One hundred and eleven times
those brows had furrowed at catastrophes
tumbling out of the morning paper
and etching themselves into his skin.

The answer was always *Fa-las-teen*—
a place I hadn't been to, an event still unfolding.
Its Arabic rhyme-sisters: *ba-sa-teen*—
gardens I could only read about at school
and *fa-sa-teen*—
dresses that made me think of a party
everyone else had been invited to.

Not me and not my father
who would answer questions
but didn't really want to talk about it.

At the US Customs desk it was more complicated.
The agent's question had a serrated edge.

How long are you planning to stay?

My father's one hundred and eleven
glistened like the rain collecting
on the windows of SeaTac airport.

Makes me wonder today
how they train customs agents.
Do they tell them stories of how
people earn their passports,

what it takes to stand in the line
where you wait for the *"Welcome home"*
instead of the scarlet letters,
precarious vocabulary of entry visas?

Makes me wonder if the agent could have imagined
that same Palestinian younger,
in pressed shirt and polished shoes,
tucked between clusters of Jericho bananas
in a pickup truck scraping a path across the desert—

one hundred and eleven flies
coursing over his sweltering frame,
one hundred and eleven thousand
stones under the tires jostling the cargo,
one hundred and eleven million degrees
of molten sunlight ravaging his mind.

Makes me wonder if the agent could imagine
the parade of nights alone in foreign cities,
the clamor of a history dissolving in the rain?

If the agent had known,
would all one hundred and eleven decibels of
I'll stay as long as I want
This is my country
that came crashing down on the counter
where my father's passport waited to receive its stamp,
would it have made more sense to him?

NAKBA

A Palestinian Cento after Neruda's "The Heights of Macchu Picchu"

Strike the old flints
to kindle ancient lamps.
Let dead lips congregate
and tell me everything
chain by chain
and link by link.

Stone within stone, and man, where was he?
Time within time, and man, where was he?
Let time exhaust all measure;
today the vacant air no longer mourns.
Your rasping voice will not come back.
You no longer exist: spider fingers, frail
threads, tangled cloth—everything you are
dropped away.

Scarred moon, menacing stone.
Night hoisted upon fingers and roots.

Love, love, do not come near the border,
a heritage of tears enshrined and buried here.
Out of the depths spin this long night to me,
show me your blood and your furrow,
speak through my speech, and through my blood
and let me cry:
hours, days and years,
blind ages, stellar centuries.

PRIVILEGE

After you die
your bones
will travel
blessed and sanctified
to rest in the earth
from which my house was made
from which my house was razed
wall by wall torn down
to make room
for your prayers
to be answered.

YAFA

on the shore phantom homes call
softly casting shadows
where beach umbrellas now line up
a row of candy-colored soldiers
shoulder to shoulder
facing the sea

salt of refugee tears
fuses with grains of sand
did the sea drink this sorrow

is light renewed each sunrise
or are the same strands
that lit the water as boats
tilted with their sobbing cargo
amassing now on the horizon

how far do tears travel
south of this silence on the beaches of Gaza
a million tears condense in besieged homes

time lives inside of us

how the waves rush
to the edge of what was
and return translucent
scattering seashells

when do we reach
the end of this erosion
do we fade one grain at a time
chimera of foam cresting on sand
where once there was life now
only salt
collecting in wounds

MAY FLOWERS

In early May in sunlight,
concrete homes nestle in wisteria clusters
on the hills, their colors dappled
as the brows of old women, their windows
glinting gold teeth in mouths full of story.

A rainy winter is no promise of comfort,
no respite in valleys of thirst.
A rainy winter is the bone-chill of walls
dampening, cold
sweat of cinder blocks.

This is the part of town where the houses still
lean into one another shouldering sorrows,
metal gates tarnished amber as vinegar
collecting daylight in jars on the windowsill.

This is the part of town where turquoise sky
hemmed with satellite dishes and
crowded with minarets threading
prayers in its seams
awakens again to
May on the other side of waiting.

Beyond the dreamscape of marble-floored
villas and manicured drought along the border,
the earth drinks every ounce
of rain, sends red poppies,
wild-thyme refugees
drifting across hillsides.
Beyond the dreamscape the barbed wire
curls and sinews,
languid on the low walls.

This is the part of town where girls
buy loaves of thin bread wrapped in yesterday's news
and boys chase stray cats down numberless streets.

This is the part of town where
there are always children outside,
their voices an echo of villages lost,
their kites heralding the sunset,
May flowers in the East Amman sky.

IN CASE OF EMERGENCY

This is how you open the box
when I am no longer here.

One of these might be the combination:

1975
The year you were born

1967
The year we lost the rest of our country

1936
The year your grandmother swallowed her gold coins
to hide them from the soldiers

This is how you keep yourself
safe, keep parts

of yourself in different boxes
Trust no one
with everything

1949
The year my father died

1977
The year the checkpoint taught you
the difference between your name and your passport

1999
The year the last of our olives were uprooted
and the wall obscured Jerusalem

This is how you know it will end:

At night, the windows of the city become mirrors,
a key recalls the shape of its doorway,
the stones of this earth
nestle in young hands.

WHEN THE SKY IS NO LONGER A WOMB FOR PRAYERS

Besieged inside your throat
prayers hum over whistles
and shrieks—the long howl
puncturing what was.

Silence is the first casualty.
You no longer fear the clamor,
not because you are brave, but
because you've learned that death arrives
noiselessly, hovering
in the bowels of a missile,

that the clamor means
you are alive and someone else is dying.
You note the bleakness of your own heart
wanting to live in spite of this.

Lena Khalaf Tuffaha is an American writer of Palestinian, Syrian, and Jordanian heritage. She writes poetry, essays, and literary translations. Her first book of poems, *Water & Salt*, is published by Red Hen Press. She translated Iraqi poet Faiza Sultan's book *I Am a Guest on This Earth* (Dar Safi Press 2015). Her essays have been published in *Al-Ahram Weekly*, the *Seattle Times*, and *Kenyon Review Online*. Lena's poems have been nominated for the Pushcart Prize and *Best of the Net*, and her poems have been published in journals including *Barrow Street, Blackbird, Diode, the Rumpus, River's Edge*, and *Sukoon*. She is proud to be a Hedgebrook alum and an MFA candidate at the Rainier Writing Workshop. She lives in Redmond, Washington with her family.

Publications by Two Sylvias Press:

The Daily Poet: Day-By-Day Prompts For Your Writing Practice
by Kelli Russell Agodon and Martha Silano (Print and eBook)

The Daily Poet Companion Journal (Print)

Fire On Her Tongue: An Anthology of Contemporary Women's Poetry
edited by Kelli Russell Agodon and Annette Spaulding-Convy (Print and eBook)

The Poet Tarot and Guidebook: A Deck Of Creative Exploration (Print)

Arab in Newsland, Winner of the 2016 Two Sylvias Press Chapbook Prize
by Lena Khalaf Tuffaha (Print and eBook)

The Blue Black Wet of Wood
by Carmen R. Gillespie (Print and eBook)

Fire Girl: Essays on India, America, and the In-Between
by Sayantani Dasgupta (Print and eBook)

Blood Song
by Michael Schmeltzer (Print and eBook)

Naming The No-Name Woman,
Winner of the 2015 Two Sylvias Press Chapbook Prize
by Jasmine An (Print and eBook)

Community Chest
by Natalie Serber (Print)

Phantom Son: A Mother's Story of Surrender
by Sharon Estill Taylor (Print and eBook)

What The Truth Tastes Like
by Martha Silano (Print and eBook)

landscape/heartbreak
by Michelle Peñaloza (Print and eBook)

Earth, Winner of the 2014 Two Sylvias Press Chapbook Prize
by Cecilia Woloch (Print and eBook)

The Cardiologist's Daughter
by Natasha Kochicheril Moni (Print and eBook)

She Returns to the Floating World
by Jeannine Hall Gailey (Print and eBook)

Hourglass Museum
by Kelli Russell Agodon (eBook)

Cloud Pharmacy
by Susan Rich (eBook)

Dear Alzheimer's: A Caregiver's Diary & Poems
by Esther Altshul Helfgott (eBook)

Listening to Mozart: Poems of Alzheimer's
by Esther Altshul Helfgott (eBook)

Crab Creek Review 30th Anniversary Issue featuring Northwest Poets
edited by Kelli Russell Agodon and Annette Spaulding-Convy (eBook)

Please visit Two Sylvias Press (www.twosylviaspress.com) for information on purchasing our print books, eBooks, writing tools, and for submission guidelines for our annual chapbook prize. Two Sylvias Press also offers editing services and manuscript consultations.

Created with the belief that great writing is good for the world.

two sylvias press

Visit us online: www.twosylviaspress.com